To Wren, for all the dreams
to come – EBH

May your curiosity and fascination with
the world never fade away – OD

© 2025 Quarto Publishing plc
Text © 2025 Edward Brooke-Hitching
Illustrations © 2025 Oksana Drachkovska

Edward Brooke-Hitching has asserted his right
to be identified as the author of this work.
Oksana Drachkovska has asserted her right
to be identified as the illustrator of this work.

Editor: Alice Hobbs
Senior Editor: Molly Mead
Designers: Ella Tomkins and Sarah Chapman-Suire
Creative Director: Malena Stojić
Associate Publisher: Holly Willsher
Senior Production Controller: Nikki Ingram

First published in 2025 by words & pictures,
an imprint of The Quarto Group.
1 Triptych Place, London,
SE1 9SH, United Kingdom.
T (0)20 7700 6700 F (0)20 7700 8066
www.quarto.com

EEA Representation, WTS Tax d.o.o., Žanova ulica 3, 4000 Kranj, Slovenia

No part of this publication may be reproduced, stored in a retrieval system,
or transmitted in any form, or by any means, electrical, mechanical,
photocopying, recording or otherwise, without the prior written permission
of the publisher or a licence permitting restricted copying. In the United
Kingdom such licences are issued by the Copyright Licensing Agency,
Third Floor, 6 Hays Lane, London, SE1 2HB
All rights reserved.

Warning: this book is for general information purposes only. Attempting stunts
referred to in the book is dangerous and could result in serious injury.
Do not try this at home.

A catalogue record for this book is available from the British Library.
ISBN: 978-1-83600-455-4
Manufactured in Guangdong, China TT062025
9 8 7 6 5 4 3 2 1

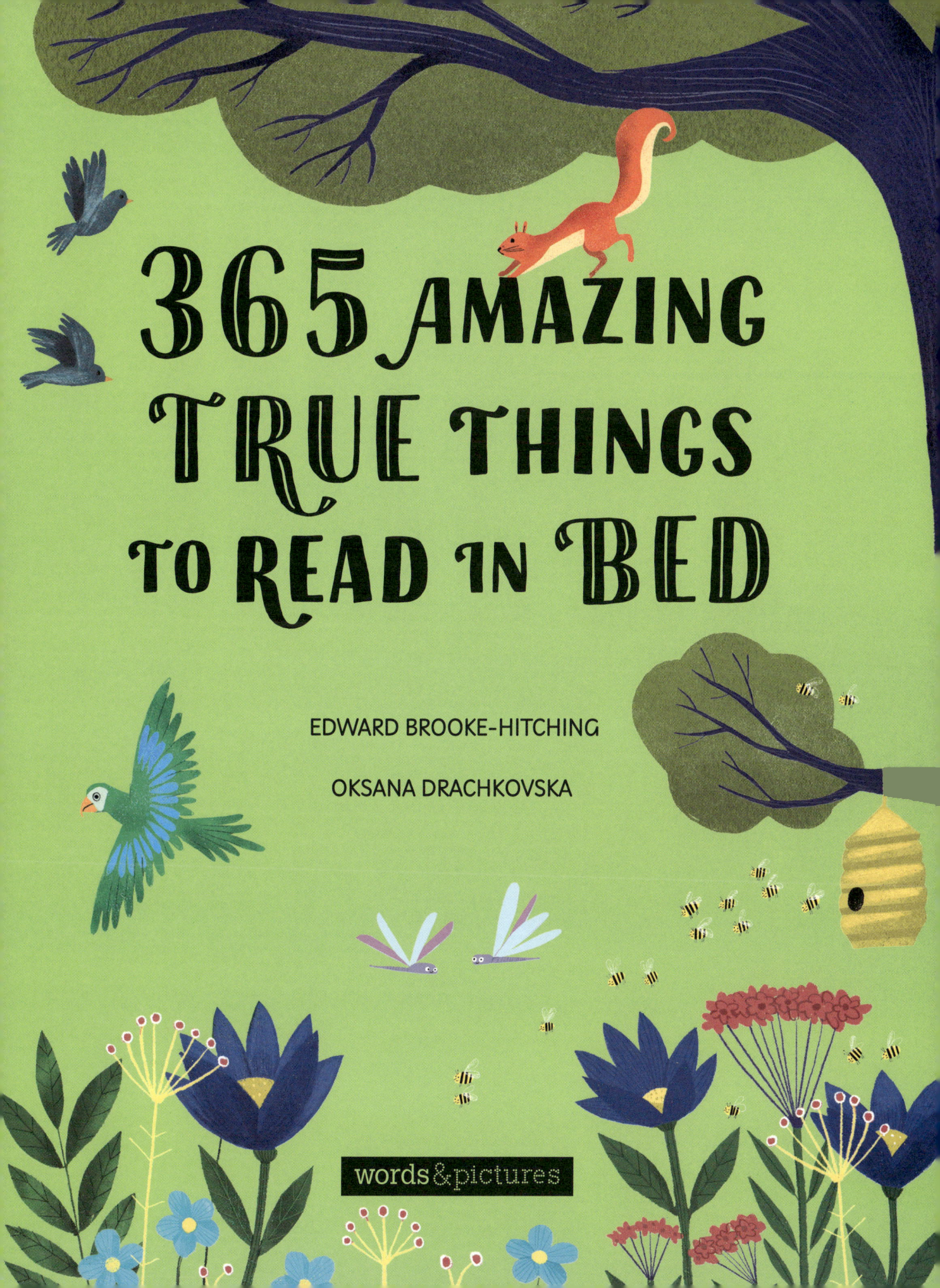

A Note from the Author

This is a book that can be read anywhere – in the car, on the loo, in the bath, up a tree or even that place you go to hide when you don't want to help with the washing-up. But the *best* place to read this book is in bed.

You probably think of your bed as a pretty boring place to be. After all, you go there to do literally *nothing* until you fall asleep – 365 times a year. But maybe you're like me. Maybe at the end of the day, as you slide under the covers and rest your head on the cool pillow . . . you find that you're still wide awake. Maybe, as you lie there waiting to drift off, you realize that you're not quite ready to fall asleep. You want one more interesting thing to look at, one more weird fact, one more terrific tale. In which case this book is here to help. Because bedtime doesn't have to be the end of the adventure. Sometimes it's just the beginning . . .

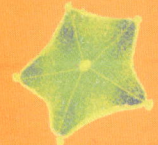

But first, a WARNING: the content of this book will *fill* your dreams. You're about to encounter creatures, characters and customs that you won't believe really exist. The wacky wonders on these pages will show you just how big, beautiful and absolutely bananas our world – our *universe* – can be. It's a place where anything is possible.

Here come answers to questions you didn't have before. Where in the world can you swim in a fluorescent pink lake (page 78) or climb rainbow-coloured mountains (page 61)? Which country has more ancient pyramids than Egypt (page 13) and where does it rain diamonds (page 7)? Why would you keep a dog up your sleeve (page 60) and where can you find fish that live in trees (page 29)? And who exactly was William Johnson Hippopotamus (page 43)?

Let this book fuel your dreams and fill your imagination with stories that burst like fireworks from its pages. When you wake up tomorrow, you'll be ready and revving like a race car to make some great discoveries of your own. But above all, remember the most amazing thing about this book: everything you're about to read is *absolutely* true . . .

1

Every ten seconds, somewhere in the universe, a massive star EXPLODES. This is called a **supernova**. It happens when a star starts to collapse in on itself during the last stage of its life. It takes just a few seconds for stars eight times the size of our Sun to implode in this way.

2

You are made of stars! All the elements in your body – the carbon, nitrogen, oxygen and other atoms that make up human beings – were originally created billions of years ago when ancient stars went supernova and exploded. The explosions sprayed stardust all around the universe, which eventually turned into YOU.

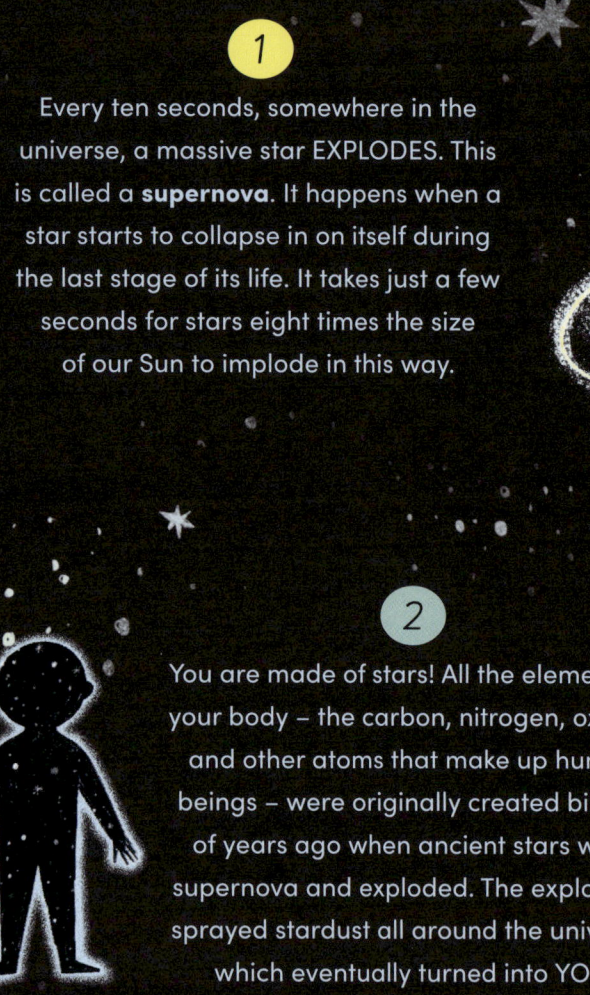

3

Saturn is the only planet in the solar system that is less **dense** than water. Theoretically, if you could find a bathtub big enough, Saturn would float in it!

4

On some of Saturn's moons there are volcanoes that erupt with ice, not **lava**. Scientists are really excited about this because where there's water, even if it's frozen, there could be life too . . .

5

On planets other than Earth, it doesn't rain water. On Jupiter, Saturn, Neptune and Uranus, for example, it rains diamonds! Lightning storms turn gas in the atmospheres of these planets into soot, and the carbon it contains hardens into diamonds. (So if you ever get the chance to visit these planets, remember to take a *big* empty suitcase with you . . .).

6

There are different types of weather on the Sun, just like on Earth – even rainstorms! It's not rain made of water, but droplets of a superhot gas called **plasma**. This 'rain' falls incredibly fast (200,000 kilometres per hour), and each droplet is the size of the island of Ireland!

7

The tallest mountain in the whole of our solar system is on Mars. It's an ancient volcano called Olympus Mons that is about two and a half times as tall as Mount Everest, Earth's highest mountain. It's also about the same width as France.

8

Although Mars is known as the red planet, its sunsets actually glow a gorgeous blue.

9

Venus's atmosphere is so thick and dense that it would be impossible for you to walk on the planet's surface. The pressure all over your body would feel the same as having a small car sitting on your thumbnail – ouch! You'd need a superstrong vessel or suit to stop yourself from being completely squished.

10

The planet Venus spins so slowly that, theoretically, you could stroll across it at the same speed as the Sun appears to move through its sky. This means that you could watch a sunset for as long as you could keep walking.

11

On Venus, instead of rainbows there are **glories** – huge multicoloured rings of light that hover in the sky when sunlight is scattered by cloud droplets.

12

Here on Earth, you might sometimes see a strange glowing ribbon of purple and green light in the night sky above Canada, Alaska, Northern Europe, New Zealand or Australia. Scientists call it STEVE (Strong Thermal Emission Velocity Enhancement).

13

In the UK and Ireland, the Plough is the nickname for the shape of the seven brightest stars in the **constellation** Ursa Major (or the Great Bear). In the US and Canada it's called the Big Dipper.

14

It's impossible to burp in space! You need **gravity** to separate gas from the food and liquid in your stomach. This means, however, you might cough both up together, something which astronauts politely call a 'wet burp'.

15

Have you ever wondered what space smells like? The astronaut Don Pettit described a pleasant 'sweet-smelling' odour. Other astronauts have compared it to burning metal, walnuts, brake pads or burnt almond cookies. Buzz Aldrin and Neil Armstrong said it smelt like gunpowder.

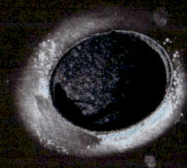

16

Some scientists have pondered the question of what space tastes like. We know that at least one part of space tastes like raspberries. In 2009, astronomers in Spain studied a huge dust cloud at the centre of the Milky Way, known as Sagittarius B2, with their telescope. One of the chemicals they identified was ethyl formate, which gives raspberries their flavour.

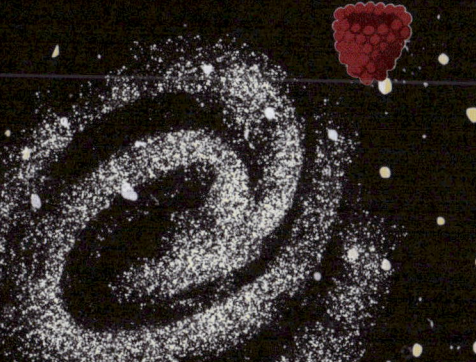

17

A tiny part of the warm rays hitting your skin on a sunny day is made from light sent by distant stars, and even **black holes**, beyond our **galaxy**.

18

In 1977, NASA sent two spacecraft called *Voyager 1* and *Voyager 2* to explore deep space. In case they found aliens, each spacecraft carried a gold-plated record with recordings from Earth. These included sounds, music, and greetings in 55 languages. Some of the sounds included waves, rain, laughter, frogs, birds, dogs, trains and cars.

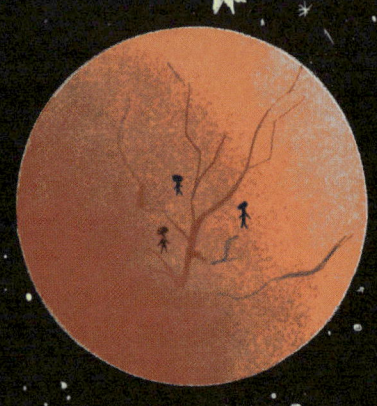

19

In 1907, an American astronomer called Percival Lowell looked at Mars through his telescope and saw lines on the planet's surface that he decided must be canals made by aliens. He wrote three books about what kind of alien life might be living on Mars. It was later discovered that he had probably made a mistake: the lines he saw were actually just the reflection in the telescope lens of the blood vessels in his own eye – oops!

20

At the same time that dinosaurs walked the Earth, there were volcanoes erupting on the Moon.

21

In Ancient Mesopotamia, a region that is now part of Iraq, kings were so terrified of lunar eclipses that they would hire a body double to take their place for a few days. This was because people believed that eclipses were a sign that the gods were angry – and angry gods might want to kill the king. The real king would hide away until the eclipse had passed, while the substitute king took control.

22

Astronauts can't whistle inside their spacesuits. The air pressure is much lower than normal atmospheric pressure, which means there aren't enough air molecules to blow with your lips and make the sound.

23

The Vikings believed that there were wolves in the sky that chased the Sun and the Moon, trying to eat them. When a solar eclipse happened and the world went dark because the Moon blocked the Sun's light, they thought it was because one of the wolves had successfully swallowed the Sun.

24

Billions of years ago, Mars had a water cycle just like Earth – there were oceans of water, ice was trapped in glaciers, and it rained. It's thought that oceans were created when asteroids containing water crashed into Mars. Although scientists have found evidence of water in the planet's rocks and atmosphere, images sent to Earth by remote-controlled **rovers** show an incredibly dry and dusty landscape.

25

Humans have left at least 181,000 kilograms of stuff on the Moon, including a photograph, a hammer, golf balls, a feather and 96 bags of human waste – meaning vomit, urine and poo!

26

Did you know our planet could sing? Scientists have discovered that Earth makes a humming sound, though it's too low for humans to hear. They think it might be caused by the pounding of ocean waves sending vibrations through the planet. This is one of the oldest sounds in the world . . .

27

In 1926, one-fifth of the entire population of Poland signed a birthday card for the USA to celebrate its 150 years of independence. The card had 5.5 million signatures.

28

The Guinness World Record for the oldest cat was set in 2005 when Creme Puff died in Texas, USA, at the age of 38. Creme Puff's owner kept her entertained with a home cinema that played animal documentaries, and fed her eggs, turkey bacon and coffee with cream each day.

29

In some countries, such as Spain, it's tradition to gently tug a person's earlobe on their birthday. The number of tugs matches their age.

30

When the Aztec Empire began in 1428, Oxford University was already at least 330 years old.

31

When Fredric J. Baur, the man who designed the packaging for Pringles, died in 2008, some of his ashes were put in a Pringles tube and placed in his burial plot. Similarly, at the funeral of the inventor of Doritos, Arch West, in 2011, mourners sprinkled a few of the snacks over his urn before it was buried.

32

Egypt is famous for having around 118 pyramids, but its fellow North African country of Sudan has even more – about twice as many have been discovered there so far.

33

The Ancient Egyptians didn't know that the world was a sphere, they thought it was a flat disc. As a result, they believed that punishment for the wicked after death would be to walk upside down with their feet on the underside of this disc. Even worse, their digestion would go in reverse and they would poo from their mouths!

34

In Ancient Egypt marshmallows were reserved for the gods and the royal family.

35

Egyptian pharaohs were cared for by a team of medics, with each member of the team specializing in a different disease or part of the body. One of these doctors was the *Neru Pehut*, which translates as 'Guardian of the Pharaoh's Bottom'.

It's the knees for me!

I've got the arms!

I'm on toe duty!

That leaves me with the bottom . . .

36

King Ramses IV, an Egyptian pharaoh who died in 1160 BCE, was buried with raw onions placed over his eyes and on other parts of his body. Researchers think this is because Egyptians believed that onions were magical and that their powerful smell could help the dead breathe again.

37

Emperor Honorius, who ruled Ancient Rome from CE 393 to 423, banned trousers as he thought that only **barbarians** would wear something so uncivilized.

38

Astronauts on the International Space Station sometimes wear the same underpants for up to a week straight. As part of an experiment, Japanese astronaut Koichi Wakata wore the same pair of hi-tech undies for a whole *month*.

39

About 2.5 per cent of your body is made of different metals – including traces of gold!

40

Babies have more bones than adults. The average adult human has 206 bones, but a baby has around 300. This is because a lot of these fuse together to make larger bones as children grow and develop.

41

Princess Alexandra of Bavaria (who lived from 1826 to 1875) believed that she had swallowed a glass piano when she was young. She was sure that the giant instrument was still inside her stomach and could break at any moment.

42

King Charles VI of France (who lived from 1368 to 1422) was convinced that he was made of glass. He always wore clothes with iron rods to protect himself and he didn't let anyone come near him in case their touch would cause him to shatter into pieces.

43

There are no muscles at all in your fingers and thumbs. Instead they contain **tendons**, which are attached to muscles in other parts of the hand.

44

In the West Asian country of Oman, after men shake hands they might also rub their noses together as a greeting.

Humans are born smarter by three IQ points every decade, and no one knows why. Maybe in a few decades' time someone will be clever enough to work it out!

46

Around the world, winds have their own local names. In Egypt there is the dry, hot *khamsin*, in France there's the *mistral* and in South Africa there's the *cape doctor*, which gets its name from the idea that it's good for your health. In Australia the *brickfielder* blows red dust all over Sydney and in Germany there's the *cat's nose*, which is named after the small round shape of the cloud that forms in front of it.

In some European languages, such as Italian, French and Portuguese, people call their toes 'feet fingers'.

48

You can speak at least one word in every language on Earth – the word 'huh' is understood everywhere.

49

The longest word in the world is found in the English language. At 189,819 letters long, it would take you three hours to pronounce. But don't worry, it's very unlikely you (or anyone, really) will ever have to say it out loud. It's a chemistry term for all the ingredients of a **protein** called titin. So that you can have a try, here's the first tiny part: Methionylthreonylthreonylglutaminylarginyl . . . given up yet?

50

There are thousands of men in Sweden called Love – in 2022, 328 babies were given the name.

51

The King Abdulaziz Festival, which is held every year in Saudi Arabia, is a beauty pageant for camels. Awards are given to only the most beautiful of the thousands of camels that compete. The judges look for slender necks, round humps and long eyelashes.

52

Every August in the Greek village of Markopoulo, Cephalonia, Christians bring snakes to church in honour of the Virgin Mary. Some people believe that many years ago she protected Christians on the island by sending snakes to scare away a band of pirates. This tradition is a show of thanks.

53

There's an island in the Pacific Ocean called Palmerston Island. Despite it being nearly 16,000 kilometres away from the UK, the English spoken there has a Gloucestershire lilt to it. This is because the 60 or so residents that live there today are descendants of a West Country sailor named William Marsters who arrived on the island in 1863.

54

Today, Russia's Wrangel Island in the Arctic Ocean is known as the 'island of polar bears', but about 3,700 years ago it had different inhabitants. The last woolly mammoths on Earth lived there, trapped on the island by rising sea levels.

55

On the South Pacific island of Fiji there is a tradition that if a young man wants to marry his beloved, he has to give his future father-in-law the tooth of a sperm whale as a gift.

56
An Ancient Greek man would let a woman know that he loved her by tossing apples in her direction.

57
Vikings would declare their devotion to one another by gathering a bouquet of purple flowers and sticking them in their love interest's face.

58
In Austria, 200 years ago, when a woman wanted a man to dance with her she would put a slice of apple under her armpit and then give it to him. If he liked her too, he would take a bite, and together they would dance all night.

59
The yellow-billed oxpecker is a tiny Sub-Saharan African bird that likes to feed on the bugs crawling in the hair of giraffes. At night it sleeps in the giraffe's hairy armpit.

60
Yawning budgies make other budgies yawn.

61
Hummingbird eggs are the size of jelly beans.

62
Scientists aren't sure why we yawn.

63
The smallest droplets in a human sneeze can travel up to 61 metres.

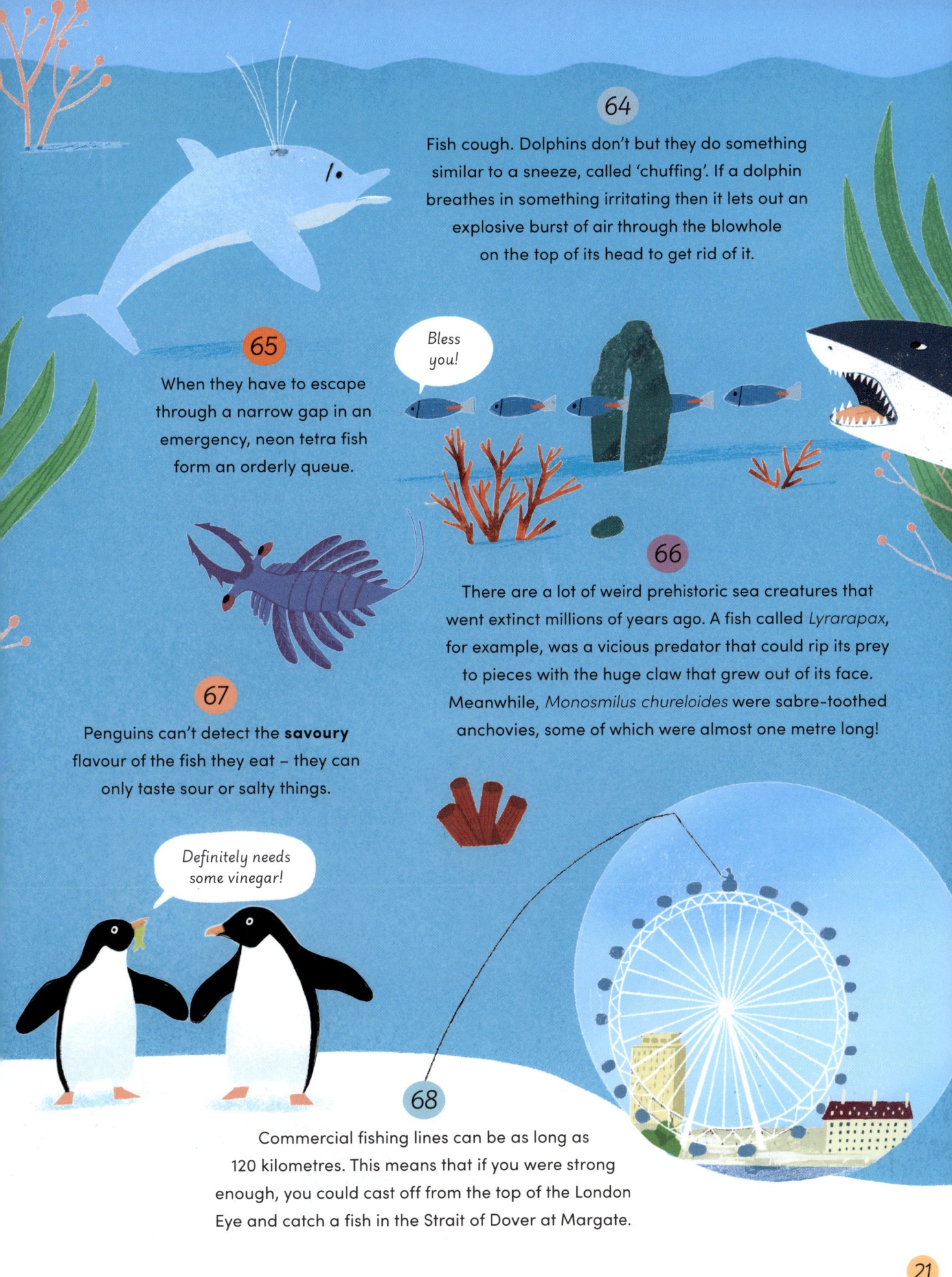

64

Fish cough. Dolphins don't but they do something similar to a sneeze, called 'chuffing'. If a dolphin breathes in something irritating then it lets out an explosive burst of air through the blowhole on the top of its head to get rid of it.

Bless you!

65

When they have to escape through a narrow gap in an emergency, neon tetra fish form an orderly queue.

66

There are a lot of weird prehistoric sea creatures that went extinct millions of years ago. A fish called *Lyrarapax*, for example, was a vicious predator that could rip its prey to pieces with the huge claw that grew out of its face. Meanwhile, *Monosmilus chureloides* were sabre-toothed anchovies, some of which were almost one metre long!

67

Penguins can't detect the **savoury** flavour of the fish they eat – they can only taste sour or salty things.

Definitely needs some vinegar!

68

Commercial fishing lines can be as long as 120 kilometres. This means that if you were strong enough, you could cast off from the top of the London Eye and catch a fish in the Strait of Dover at Margate.

69 Dolphins can't smell.

70 Platypuses sweat milk. They don't have teats to feed their young, so their milk oozes out of glands and into grooves on their skin.

71 If you're ever looking for a manatee's nipples, you can find them in its armpits – or should that be flipper-pits?

72 There was a frog that was so big it could eat small dinosaurs. Scientists call it *Beelzebufo* – which means 'the frog from hell' – and it lived about 65 to 70 million years ago. It had a bite that was twice as powerful as a human's.

73 The world's tiniest frog, commonly known as the 'flea toad' of Brazil, is smaller than a bluebottle fly.

74

For Dumbo, the baby elephant from the Disney animation, to fly in real life, he'd have to zoom at over 320 kilometres per hour and his ears would have to be over 47 metres wide (almost the length of an Olympic swimming pool!).

75

An African elephant can use its feet to 'hear'. Vibrations from the ground are transmitted through bones in its front legs and shoulders into its middle ear.

Pardon?

76

Elephants are amazing long-distance swimmers, with some having been seen paddling for a distance of 48 kilometres. They are surprisingly **buoyant** and use their trunk like a snorkel to breathe easily as they go.

77
The first animals to successfully return from a mission to space were two dogs called Belka and Strelka, who were launched on 19 August 1960 on the Soviet spacecraft *Sputnik 5*.

78
In 1973 the first spider's webs were made in space after NASA sent two spiders, Arabella and Anita, to the USA's space station. They wanted to see if lower gravity affected their building skills. Although it took the spiders time to adjust, they eventually built webs that were much more complicated and delicate than those made on Earth.

79
You probably know that polar bears live in the Arctic, but did you know that all polar bears are actually Irish? They descend from brown bears that lived in Ireland during the last ice age – between 38,000 and 10,000 years ago. Polar bears are also not white: their fur is translucent and hollow and their skin underneath is black. They look white because their fur is reflecting light. (Also, most polar bears are born as twins.)

80
Alligators wait motionless in water with twigs perched on their noses to lure birds who are looking for things to build their nests with.

SNAP!

81
The Chinese giant panda is no longer classed as endangered. There were only 1,000 pandas in the wild in the 1970s, but today there are almost 2,000.

82
In 2014, a Chinese newspaper reported that a female giant panda had tricked her zookeepers into thinking she was pregnant. They suspected it was so she would receive extra buns, fruits and bamboo, and a nice air-conditioned room to herself.

83
Pandas poo 40 times per day.

84

Northen Collard Lemmings have poo that glows in ultraviolet light. Some scientists think this is why they poo underground – because they don't want predators to see it and come after them.

85

Bombardier beetles kill attackers by using their bottoms to spray them with chemicals that are almost as hot as boiling water.

86

Centuries ago, a face mask made from bird poo was developed in Japan. The beauty treatment is called *uguisu no fun* and uses nightingale poo. It claims to improve skin tone and moisture levels and is still offered in spas today.

87

The Arabic name for hamster translates as 'Mr Saddlebags'. Golden (Syrian) hamsters were given the name because of their ability to stuff their cheeks with food.

88

Chipmunks can hold so much food in their cheek pouches that they can stretch to the same size as the chipmunk's entire body.

89

As orangutans go to sleep, they blow raspberries at each other.

Take that!

90

According to historian Herodotus, a revolution in Ancient Egypt was started with a fart. The pharaoh Apries sent a messenger to a rebel named Amasis, ordering him to surrender. Amasis replied by farting and telling the messenger to "take that back to Apries". The two went to war and Amasis won, declaring himself the new pharaoh in 570 BCE.

91

In 18th-century England, the slang word for hens was 'cacklers'. And eggs were called 'cackling farts'.

92

Chickens will lay more eggs if you play them music. Some studies have shown that hens are most productive when listening to rock music, while others suggest classical music is best.

93

The biggest goldfish ever recorded was called 'the Carrot' – and she wouldn't have fitted in a regular goldfish bowl. The Carrot was caught in a lake in France in 2022. She was bright orange and weighed 30.5 kilograms, about the same weight and size as a one-year-old German shepherd dog!

94

Around 70 per cent of the white sand on the beaches of Hawaii and the Caribbean is made of parrotfish poo! Most of this fish's food lives on or inside coral, so they end up ingesting and gnawing down on the coral's crunchy outer layer and pooing it out as sand. Just one adult parrotfish can poo out over a tonne of white sand in a year.

95

The African tigerfish can leap out of the water and grab birds in mid-air.

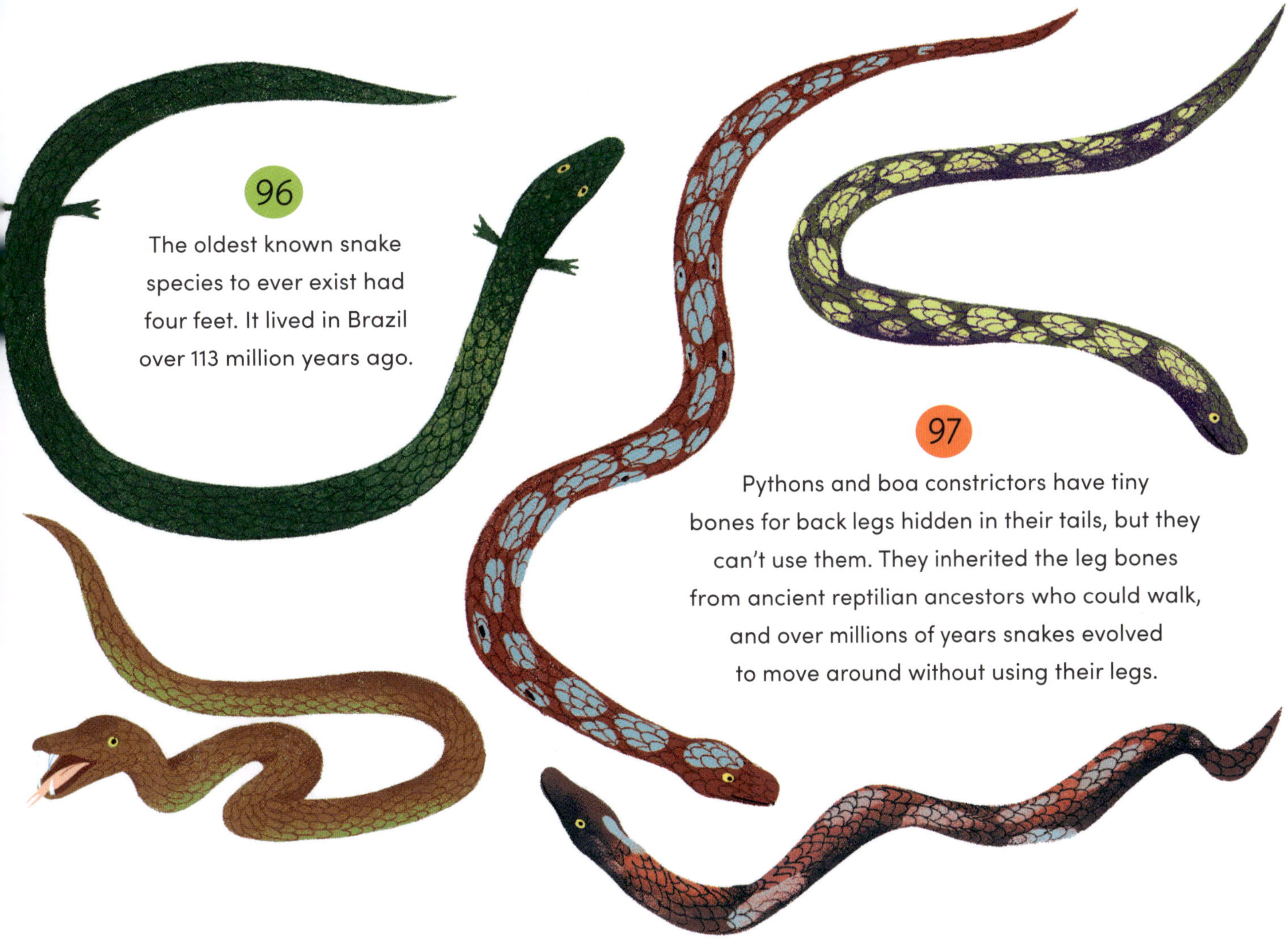

96

The oldest known snake species to ever exist had four feet. It lived in Brazil over 113 million years ago.

97

Pythons and boa constrictors have tiny bones for back legs hidden in their tails, but they can't use them. They inherited the leg bones from ancient reptilian ancestors who could walk, and over millions of years snakes evolved to move around without using their legs.

98

The tripod fish has three rigid fin 'legs' that it uses to stand on the bottom of the ocean and 'kick' approaching prey into its mouth.

99

While some types of fish can stand on the ocean floor using fins like legs, others can walk on land. Mudskippers, which are about 30 cm long, can live out of the water for several days. They can move across the ground using their fins and tail and even climb **mangrove** trees.

100
Seahorses are unique in the animal kingdom as it's the males that get pregnant, not the females. They can give birth to over 1,000 babies at once.

I really need a nanny!

101
Whale milk is as thick as toothpaste.

102
Sharks are older than trees. The earliest type of shark lived 450 million years ago, whereas the first trees did not evolve for another 80 million years. Sharks had already been on Earth for 220 million years when the first dinosaurs appeared.

103
By looking at fossils, scientists have discovered that fish developed finger bones 380 million years ago. It's thanks to these fish, and millions of years of **evolution**, that humans have hands!

104

It's hard to tell from just seeing their fins poke out of the water, but orcas (otherwise known as killer whales) are HUGE – an adult orca can reach eight metres long and weigh up to five tonnes (about the same length and weight as two big cars).

105

The title of 'longest animal in the world' should probably go to a creature you've likely never heard of: the siphonophore. In 2020, one of these bizarre sea creatures was discovered off the coast of Western Australia – it was about 45 metres long! They look like long strings made of jelly and wind themselves in huge circles underwater. Beware though, they can sting.

106

One of the most famous animals in Japan was LaLa, a king penguin belonging to the Nishimoto family. Rescued in the 1990s, he lived in his own air-conditioned room, and was seen every day walking to the local fish market wearing a backpack to collect fresh fish for himself and his foster family.

107

Just like domestic cats, lions can get hairballs – the difference is that a lion's hairball can be as large as a rugby ball.

108

The largest leech ever discovered was an Amazon giant leech found by Dr Roy Sawyer in French Guiana in the 1970s. He named it Grandma Moses. She was 45 cm long (one and a half times a regular school ruler) and had 750 babies.

109

Hippopotamuses are one of the most vicious animals in the world, but there's another reason not to get near them: they spray their dung around! They often whirl their tail like a propeller while pooing to spread their waste and mark their territory. This also helps make sure that any leeches they've squeezed out don't crawl back into their bottom.

110
An octopus has nine brains – one in each arm and another in the middle of its body.

No wonder I'm so intelligent!

111
In 2022, scientists discovered that octopuses like to tidy their home by scooping up rubbish and throwing it away.

112
Some octopuses like to decorate their homes with seashells, and if any other octopuses try to come in, they angrily throw the shells at them. When an octopus is having a *really* bad day it might punch fish as well.

113
Male lizards try to impress females by doing press-ups in front of them.

114
Lizards can't breathe and walk at the same time.

He's so strong!

Wow!

115

The pom-pom crab gets its name from its habit of carrying a round sea anemone in each of its claws and waving them like a cheerleader.

Gooooooo team!

116

Sloths can have as many as 950 different kinds of beetles and moths crawling in their fur.

117

Sloths can hold their breath underwater for 15 minutes – most humans can't hold theirs for longer than a minute.

Blub . . . blorp . . . blor . . . blorb . . .

118

Nowadays, most dragonflies have wingspans of about 5-13 cm, but we know that there were dragonflies 300 million years ago that swooped around with wingspans of around 76 cm. Scientists call them 'griffinflies'.

119

When a woodpecker hammers away at a tree, it does so in bursts to let its brain cool down. It pecks at the tree bark so fast (20 pecks a second) and so often (12,000 times a day) that if it didn't take breaks, its brain would overheat!

120

The Komodo dragon is the largest living lizard in the world, growing to three metres. It is so big that it can overpower deer, water buffalo and occasionally humans. It uses the **venom** in the saliva of its powerful bite to kill its prey.

Whoa!

121

The insect known as the praying mantis was recently discovered to have a tongue-like organ on the *outside* of its **thorax**. This lets it taste the leaves that it clings to.

122

You can make a rat giggle by tickling it, but the laugh is so high-pitched that you won't be able to hear it. Scientists discovered this in 2016 when they played all sorts of games with rats. They found that as well as enjoying being tickled, rats also love a good game of hide-and-seek.

123
Around 3.5 million years ago, a giant otter called *Enhydriodon omoensis* roamed the earth. It weighed 200 kilograms and was the size of a lion.

124
Ostriches have four kneecaps. Humans have two, but some people's are split, like Andy Murray. Despite this challenge, he still became a tennis world champion!

125
Starfish have hundreds of feet but no brain.

126
In 1252, King Henry III of England was given a polar bear by King Haakon IV Haakonsson of Norway. It lived at the Tower of London, where it was given a long leash so that it could swim and catch fish in the River Thames.

127

King Charles III has an Aston Martin car that runs on a mixture of white wine and cheese (otherwise known as **biofuel**) instead of petrol.

128

A hundred years ago, the keepers at London Zoo used camels to pull their lawnmowers. Horses helped too, but their hooves made dents in the turf so they were given leather boots to wear.

129

Camel milk is closer to human milk than cow's milk and is higher in some vitamins and minerals. Some nomadic Bedouin people who live in the deserts of West Asia survive for weeks at a time on camel milk and dates alone.

130

Houseflies buzz in the musical key of F major. If you play a scale in that key on a musical instrument, you'll be duetting with them.

131

Alpine bumblebees can fly at altitudes of 9,000 metres, which is higher than Mount Everest.

132

Bees in a room will drop to the ground the moment you turn all the lights off.

133

In 2017, scientists used sensitive microphones to discover that when honeybees bump into each other inside the corridors of a hive, they make a loud 'whoop!' sound of surprise.

"Girl power!"

134
Only female bees sting.

135
Bees were sacred in Ancient Egypt, as people believed they were the tears of the sun god, Ra. It was thought that people who died sometimes returned in the form of a bee, and the sounds of bees buzzing were the voices of souls. Pharaohs were even buried with honey for the afterlife.

Awoooooooooo!

136
The grasshopper mouse is a **carnivore** that sneaks up on its prey like a cat, and howls like a wolf.

137
Scientists have counted mice sighing as often as 40 times per hour.

138
In 2015, a man named Sweet Pepper Klopek let 58 mousetraps snap on his tongue. "Thpoiler alert: they all hurt," he said afterwards. We do not suggest you copy him!

139
Some turtles can breathe through their bottoms.

140
A scorpion can have as many as 12 eyes.

141
A type of spinifex grass that grows in arid regions of Australia tastes like salt and vinegar crisps.

142
Scientists have found a type of red seaweed that tastes like bacon when fried – it also has twice the nutritional value of kale.

143
Danish scientists have made jellyfish crisps that are reported to taste like pork scratchings.

144
If you put sheep in a maze, they mostly turn left.

145
The Faroe Islands are a Danish territory in the North Atlantic Ocean. In 2016, the islanders wanted the world to see how beautiful their home was and so they used sheep to take photos. The sheep were fitted with solar-powered cameras that took photos as the animals roamed. The images were then uploaded to the internet. If you look up pictures of the Faroe Islands – you may well be looking at pictures taken by sheep!

146
Sweden has 267,570 islands, which is more than any other country in the world.

147

Scientists at the UK's University of Manchester have developed a sieve that is able to remove salt from seawater, making it safe to drink. The affordable technology could help the estimated 2.2 billion people worldwide who lack access to clean water.

148

The earliest name for a pet cat that we know of is Nedjem which means 'Sweetie'. It lived in Ancient Egypt during the reign of Thutmose III (1479–1425 BCE) and is pictured on the tomb of a priest called Puimre.

149

You can't fold a piece of A4 paper in half more than seven times . . . but you can try!

150

Captain James Cook was a famous English explorer who was the first European to land on Australia, Hawaii and New Zealand. One member of his crew was rather unusual: a goat, which he brought along on his voyage of 1768 to provide milk. 'The Well-Travelled Goat', as she was known, became a celebrity in London.

151

US President Calvin Coolidge had a pet pygmy hippo called William Johnson Hippopotamus. William fathered 18 babies that were all called Gumdrop.

152

Around 500 years ago, names for pets in England included: Nosewise, Clenche, Sturdy, Holdfast, Little Hammer (who belonged to a blacksmith) and Little Spoke (who belonged to a wagon-wheel maker). Anne Boleyn, one of the wives of King Henry VIII, had a very nosy and curious dog that she named Purkoy after the French word *pourquoi*, which means 'why'.

153

US President Theodore Roosevelt's daughter, Alice, kept a pet snake in the White House called Emily Spinach.

154

The famous English writer Thomas Hardy had a pet cat called Kiddleywinkempoops.

155

In the 18th century, the Irish author Jonathan Swift (who wrote the story *Gulliver's Travels*) invented the name Vanessa and the word yahoo. He also wrote a book about farting under the **pseudonym** the Countess of Fizzlerumpf.

156

Barbie's full name is Barbara Millicent Roberts.

157

Sonic the Hedgehog's full name is Ogilvie Maurice Hedgehog.

158

A baby porcupine is called a porcupette.

159

American bullfrogs don't sleep.

160

It is extremely rare for an octopus to be born with six legs. The first known 'hexapus' was found off the coast of Wales in 2008. Five years later an American family on holiday in Greece caught what is believed to be the second one ever found. Unfortunately they only realized how special it was after they had cooked and eaten it.

161

The oldest human fossil found in England is known as Roger. In 1993 a shinbone of an early human man who lived 480,000 years ago was found in Boxgrove, West Sussex. The remains were named after Roger Pedersen, the Danish man who discovered the bones.

162

The person with the longest ever name in history was a German-born American man who lived from 1914 to 1997. His full name was 747 letters long. Can you pronounce it? Take a deep breath!

Adolph Blaine Charles David Earl Frederick Gerald Hubert Irvin John Kenneth Lloyd Martin Nero Oliver Paul Quincy Randolph Sherman Thomas Uncas Victor William Xerxes Yancy Zeus Wolfeschlegelsteinhausenbergerdorffwelchevoralternwarengewissenhaftschaferswessenschafewarenwohlgepfleundsorgfaltigkeitbeschutzenvonangreifendurchihrraubgierigfeindewelchevoralternzwolftausendjahresvorandieerscheinenvanderersteerdemenschderraumschiffgebrauchlichtalsseinursprungvonkraftgestartseinlangefahrthinzwischensternartigraumaufdersuchenachdiesternwelchegehabtbewohnbarplanetenkreisedrehensichundwohinderneurassevonverstandigmenschlichkeitkonntefortpflanzenundsicherfreuenanlebenslanglichfreudeundruhemitnichteinfurchtvorangreifenvonandererintelligentgeschopfsvonhinzwischensternartigraum

163

One of the longest beards in history belonged to a Bavarian man named Hans Steininger, who was the mayor of Braunau am Inn in the 1500s. His beard was so long that in order to walk he had to roll it up and tuck it into his coat. You can still see his beard on display at the local museum.

164
Walruses can get dandruff.

165
Viking King Ragnar Lothbrok was nicknamed 'Shaggy Britches' because of the hairy trousers that he wore.

166
Tiaras and high heels were worn by men before they were worn by women. In Ancient Persia (modern-day Iran) kings wore colourful headdresses called 'tiáras'. A thousand years ago, male Persian soldiers wore high-heeled shoes to help their feet stay in the stirrups when riding horses into battle.

167
Mathematicians have calculated that there are 177,147 different ways to tie a tie.

168

A pair of **prototype** Nike trainers was made in 1971 using a waffle iron to create the tread on the sole of the shoes.

169

George Washington, the first president of the United States, wore dentures (false teeth) made from the teeth of cows, elephants, hippopotamuses, walruses and . . . other people.

170

When the famous British prime minister Winston Churchill got angry, he would take out his false teeth and throw them across the room.

171

The candyfloss machine was invented by a dentist called William Morrison. It turns out even dentists like a sugary treat now and again!

172

Female mosquitoes have 47 'teeth' on their mouthparts.

173

In 1964, everyone in Sweden got very excited by a mysterious new artist called Pierre Brassau. Art reviewers were amazed by his original use of colour and shape, and several people tried to buy his paintings. But Pierre Brassau was actually a chimpanzee at the local zoo named Peter who would make paintings for his keepers in exchange for bananas.

174

One hundred years ago, an artist named Zarh Pritchard was the first person to paint while standing on the sea floor. He wore lead shoes to hold him down and used oiled waterproof canvases for his underwater landscapes.

175

Leonardo da Vinci is famous for painting the Mona Lisa, but did you know the Italian artist-inventor was also a wedding planner? He once baked a 60-metre cake made to look like a church altar, complete with hundreds of chairs. Unfortunately, rats ate everything on the night before the wedding and he had to quickly bake it all again.

176

The famous English artist J.M.W. Turner, whose paintings sell today for millions of pounds, tore a hole in one of his giant masterpieces to make a cat flap for his seven Manx cats to come in and out of his studio.

177

Wild parrots in New York City have caused massive power cuts by building their nests on electrical lines.

178

Squirrels absolutely LOVE to chew through power lines and telephone cables. In 2015, the deputy director of the US National Security Agency was asked whether computer hackers posed the biggest danger to the country's power network. He replied: "Frankly, the number-one threat experienced to date is squirrels."

179

The Large Hadron Collider is a *massive* machine that was built underground below the Switzerland-France border. It is basically a circular tunnel with a circumference of 27 kilometres in which physicists smash tiny particles together to try and answer some of the most complicated questions about how the universe was made. In 2016, the *whole thing* was shut down when a weasel bit through a power cable and broke the machine. It took several weeks to repair.

180

A female rhinoceros called Cacareco was so popular in the city of São Paulo, Brazil, that in 1959 she won the election to run the city, receiving more votes than all the politicians. Sadly it was decided that a city wouldn't work very well with a rhinoceros in charge, no matter how popular they were.

181

The people of Rabbit Hash, a town in Kentucky, USA, have chosen dogs as their mayor since 1998. Former mayors include a French Bulldog called Wilbur Beast, and Lucy Lou, a red and white Border Collie.

182

Packs of some African wild dogs will decide whether it's time to go hunting together by taking a group vote – each dog votes by sneezing.

183

Leopard wee smells like popcorn.

184

In the Second World War, an American pilot called Jack Valentine Woolams liked to play jokes on other pilots. He would put on a gorilla mask and a bowler hat, and as he flew past other pilots he would give them a little wave.

This is baaaa-rmy!

185

The first hot-air balloon flight took place on 19 September 1783 at Versailles in France. The Montgolfier brothers, Joseph and Étienne, released the balloon in front of King Louis XVI at 1 p.m. It took off into the sky, carrying its three passengers: a sheep, a duck and a cockerel. It travelled 3.5 kilometres before landing in a clearing in some woodland.

186

Hundreds of years ago, when people would have sword-fighting 'duels' against each other, there were some weird tricks to help you win. One technique was to take off your coat during the fight and use it to wrap up your opponent's sword, or simply throw it around their head.

187

Many sports that were played in the past have been abandoned because they were just too dangerous. For example, in 'balloon jumping' people attached miniature hot-air balloons to their backs and leapt into a strong wind; ice tennis was played on courts made of ice and players wore ice skates; and 'firework boxing' involved two men strapping fizzing fireworks to their bodies as they fought! Do not try this at home!

188
When they need a better view, Harris's hawks will hop up onto their friends' shoulders.

189
One of the tallest waterslides in the world is Kilimanjaro at the Aldeia das Águas resort in Brazil. At 49.9 metres high, you can hit speeds of 100 kilometres per hour going down!

190
It's easier to cross the Moon's surface by skipping than walking.

191
In the near future, you might be able to travel to cities around the world using space rockets. The journey from London to New York could take just 29 minutes!

192

Roller skates were invented by a Belgian engineer called John Joseph Merlin well over two hundred years ago. He decided to skate around a fancy party in London, while also playing his violin. Unfortunately, he skated straight into an enormous mirror, smashing it to pieces and hurting himself badly. It took a while before roller skates became popular.

193

The longest treadmill in the world is for wolves. It was built by scientists in Austria so that they could watch the wolves run together in a pack.

194

Before they were used for exercise, treadmills were used as punishment for criminals in prison.

195
The country of Lithuania has an annual baby race to see which baby is the fastest crawler.

196
Babies have 30 per cent body fat by the time they are six months old.

"Bless you!"

197
A baby can sneeze while it's still in its mother's womb.

198
Before football referees had whistles, they would wave handkerchiefs.

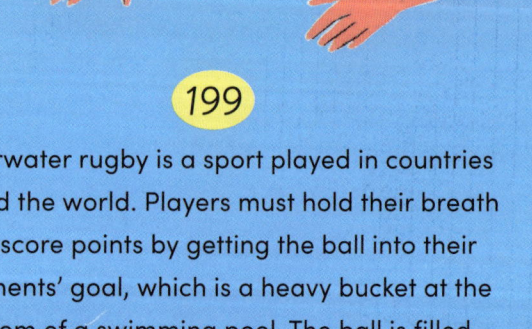

199
Underwater rugby is a sport played in countries around the world. Players must hold their breath and score points by getting the ball into their opponents' goal, which is a heavy bucket at the bottom of a swimming pool. The ball is filled with seawater to make sure it doesn't float.

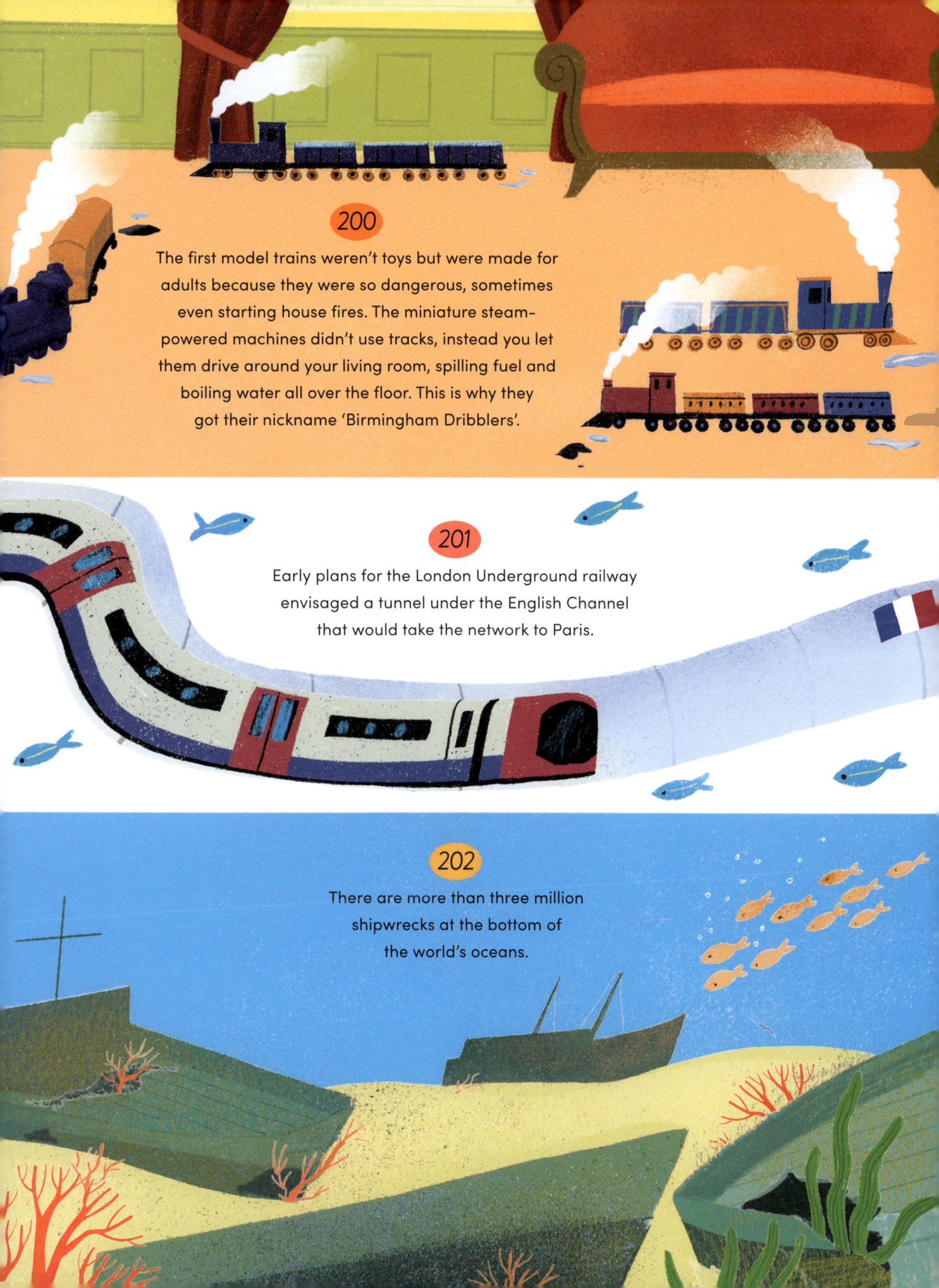

200

The first model trains weren't toys but were made for adults because they were so dangerous, sometimes even starting house fires. The miniature steam-powered machines didn't use tracks, instead you let them drive around your living room, spilling fuel and boiling water all over the floor. This is why they got their nickname 'Birmingham Dribblers'.

201

Early plans for the London Underground railway envisaged a tunnel under the English Channel that would take the network to Paris.

202

There are more than three million shipwrecks at the bottom of the world's oceans.

203

The German car maker Volkswagen sells more sausages than cars. Since 1973, a delicious spicy sausage dish called currywurst has been sold in the canteens of the German car plants.

204

In Germany during the First World War, no one was allowed to eat sausages because cow guts (used to make sausage skins) were needed to make Zeppelin airships instead.

205

In 1996, in the British village of Stokeinteignhead in Devon, a man named Neil Simmons would go out into his garden at night to hoot at owls, until finally one evening an owl hooted back at him. The two had a hooting conversation every night for over a year, until Mr Simmons discovered that the 'owl' was actually his neighbour Fred Cornes, who also thought he had been having conversations with an owl.

206

The rapper Eminem is terrified of owls.

207

The needlefish is one SCARY fish! You can find it in the Pacific Ocean – except you *really don't want* to find it. It's not its size that makes it dangerous (it only grows to about one metre), but its long jaws that form a needle-like beak. It has been known to leap out of shallow water at 60 kilometres per hour and collide with anglers and divers like an arrow. Its beak can cause deep puncture wounds which are sometimes fatal.

You're quackers!

208

You probably know that parrots can talk, but did you know that ducks can, too? This was discovered in the 1980s when an Australian musk duck named Ripper was recorded repeatedly mimicking an insult he may have heard his keeper use.

209

The theatre in the Sydney Opera House has a net above the orchestra pit. It was put up in the 1980s after a real chicken wandered off the stage during a performance and fell onto a surprised cellist.

210

In Chile, a performance in 1970 of the opera *Rigoletto* ended suddenly when the singer Louis Quilico leaned his head back to take a deep breath . . . and accidentally swallowed a pigeon feather that had drifted down from the rafters, which made him choke and then faint.

211

It is very rare to see blue fireworks because the chemicals needed are really expensive and dangerous.

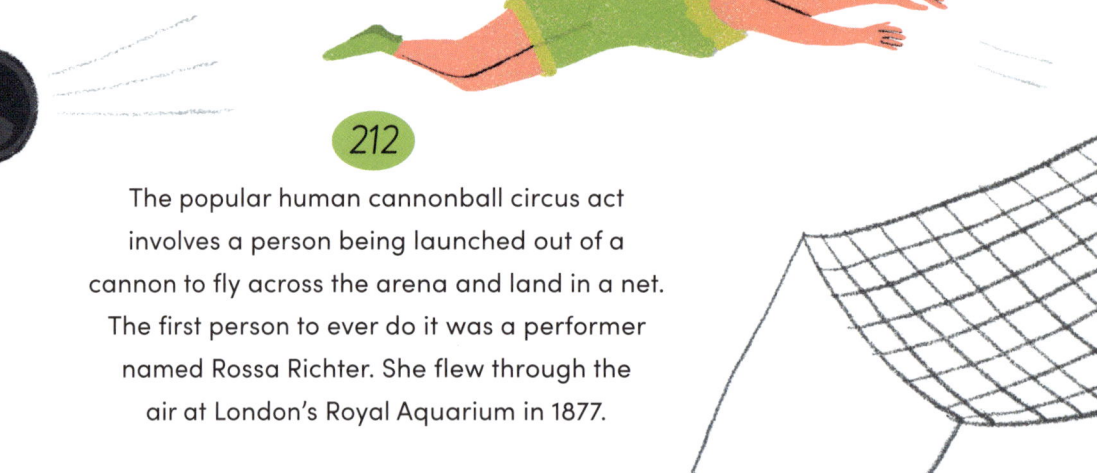

212

The popular human cannonball circus act involves a person being launched out of a cannon to fly across the arena and land in a net. The first person to ever do it was a performer named Rossa Richter. She flew through the air at London's Royal Aquarium in 1877.

213

In 2023, scientists in Colombia spotted a bird called the green honeycreeper that is half male, half female. Its colours are divided directly down the middle of its body, with its right side covered in the male blue feathers, and the left in the green plumage of the female.

214

The oldest musical instrument ever found is a flute made from the thigh bone of a prehistoric cave bear. It's 60,000 years old.

215

Every child growing up in the Russian village of Tsovkra-1 learns to walk a tightrope.

216

Visitors to Iceland can have Icelandic horses reply to their work emails for them while they enjoy their holiday. There are three horses you can choose from: Litla Stjarna Frá Hvítarholti, who "types fast, but might take a nap", Hrímnir Frá Hvammi, who is "assertive, efficient and has shiny hair", or Hekla Frá Þorkellshóli, for a "friendly" email. They have their own giant, custom-made horse-sized keyboards which they step on to write. Of course, there's a *pretty good* chance that they'll write gibberish.

217

The first vacuum cleaner was pulled by horses.

218

Daniel Wildman was an 18th-century London beekeeper who came up with a clever (and dangerous) idea to advertise his honey shop. He would ride his galloping horse through the streets standing up on the saddle, while also 'wearing' a beard of bees! People came from all over the city to watch him and buy his goods.

219

Wasps make paper. They've been making paper since before humans even existed.

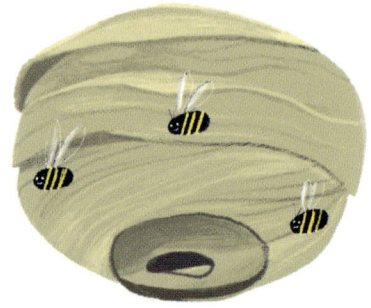

220

A 'spite house' is the name for a building that people construct purely to annoy their neighbours, sometimes by blocking their view.

221

Miniature Pekingese dogs are also called 'Sleeve Pekingese'. This comes from an old Chinese custom of keeping the little dogs cosy inside the sleeves of members of the royal household. This was also useful for self-defence – the dogs would leap out of the sleeves and chase away any would-be attackers.

222

The building of the Great Wall of China began in the seventh century BCE (over 2,700 years ago), but was only finished in 1878, which was two years after the first telephone call was made by the inventor Alexander Graham Bell.

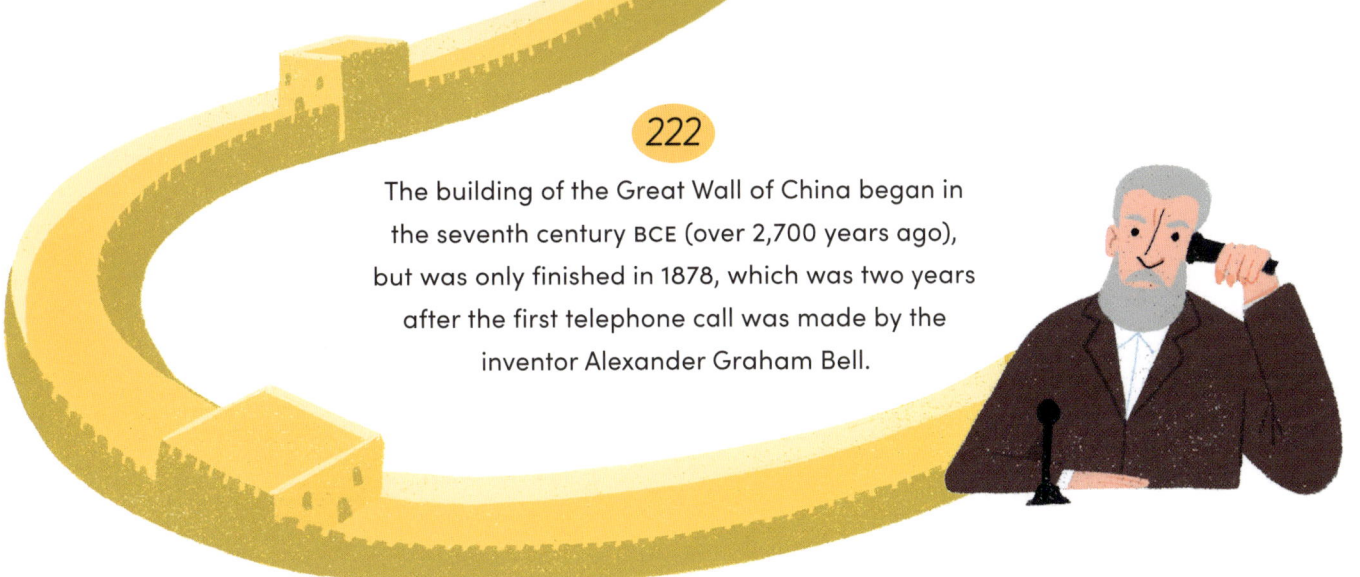

223

Until recently, the most senior officer in Thailand's Air Force was a poodle called Fufu. Fufu was the pet dog of Vajiralongkorn, the Crown Prince of Thailand. He would appear at royal dinner parties dressed in full uniform, including little black leather boots.

224

One of the most beautiful natural sights on our planet is the Rainbow Mountains at the Zhangye Danxia Geopark in China. The incredible striped landscape is made by layers of different minerals.

225

'Sahara' comes from the Arabic word ṣaḥrā meaning desert. So when we say "the Sahara Desert" we're really saying "the desert desert".

Where can I get an ice cream around here?

226

'Nile' comes from an ancient word for river, so 'the River Nile' means 'the river river'.

227

There is a city in the US state of New Mexico with the strange name of Truth or Consequences. It was originally called Hot Springs, but in 1950 it renamed itself to win a contest set by a national radio show called *Truth or Consequences*.

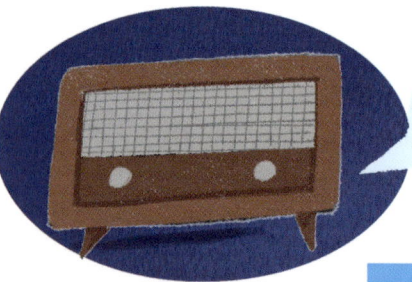

And the winner is . . . Truth or Consequences!

228

Pana po'o is a Hawaiian phrase that means "scratch your head in order to help you remember something you've forgotten".

229

The Scottish word *hurkle-durkle* means to lazily stay in bed when it's time to get up.

230

The Japanese have a special word – *tsundoku* – which is the habit of buying lots of books and letting them pile up without actually reading any of them.

231

Lagom is a useful Swedish word that means 'not too much, not too little, just the right amount'.

232

Gigil is a word in the Tagalog language of the Philippines for the overwhelming feeling of pure joy when you see something unbearably cute, like a puppy that you just have to pet.

233

Shemomedjamo is a very useful word – it's a Georgian term for when you're feeling full but you keep eating anyway because the food is so tasty.

234

In Italy they call prawn crackers *nuvole di drago*, which means 'dragon clouds'.

At JFK Airport in New York, flights are sometimes delayed while turtles are cleared from the runways.

Who's got the passports?!

236

Over a century ago in Paris, a popular thing to do was to take your pet turtle out for a walk on a lead.

237

In 2013, a father in China was worried that his unemployed 23-year-old son was spending too much time playing a computer game. So the dad hired professional gamers to kill his son's **avatar** in the hope that he'd give up and start looking for a job.

238

It took the inventor of the Rubik's Cube one month to first solve it in 1974. Today, the world record for solving the 3D puzzle is held by 22-year-old American Max Park at 3.13 seconds.

239

It's possible to win a game of Monopoly with four turns, taking just five minutes.

240

The largest game of musical chairs was played by 8,238 people in Singapore in 1989.

241

The first wallets were carried by the Ancient Greeks, who used them to keep emergency snacks handy.

Nom nom nom!

242

Bubble wrap was originally intended to be wallpaper.

243

Water balloons were created by accident when an inventor was trying to make waterproof socks!

244

Silly String was originally designed to make spray-on casts for people with broken bones.

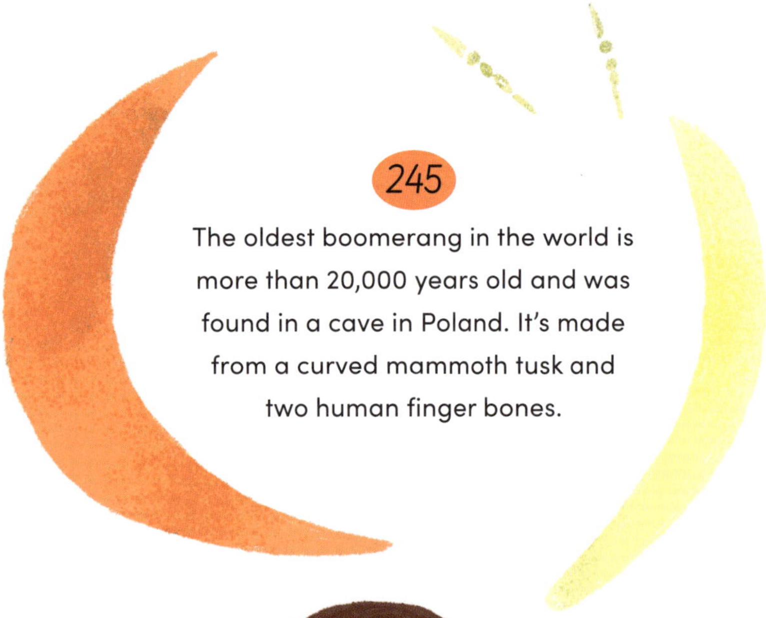

245
The oldest boomerang in the world is more than 20,000 years old and was found in a cave in Poland. It's made from a curved mammoth tusk and two human finger bones.

246
The nails of your middle fingers grow faster than the others.

247
Koala fingerprints are so similar to human fingerprints that it's hard to tell which is which.

248
When a llama is annoyed with another llama, it sticks its tongue out at them.

What's so special about his poo?!

*I love my job . . .
I love my job . . .
I love my job . . .*

249
Scientists have found a way to turn llama poo into charcoal, which they can then use to purify polluted water.

250
The world record for the most people sitting on one chair is 2,387.

251
In 2018, Italian Dimitri Panciera won the world record for most ice cream scoops piled onto a cone, when he balanced 125 balls of ice cream in one go.

252
The record for the longest thumbnail is 197.8 cm.

253
A man named Charles Osborne had hiccups non-stop for 68 years, from 1922 to 1990.

254

The British Library has so many books that even if you looked at five every day, it would take you over 80,000 years to see them all.

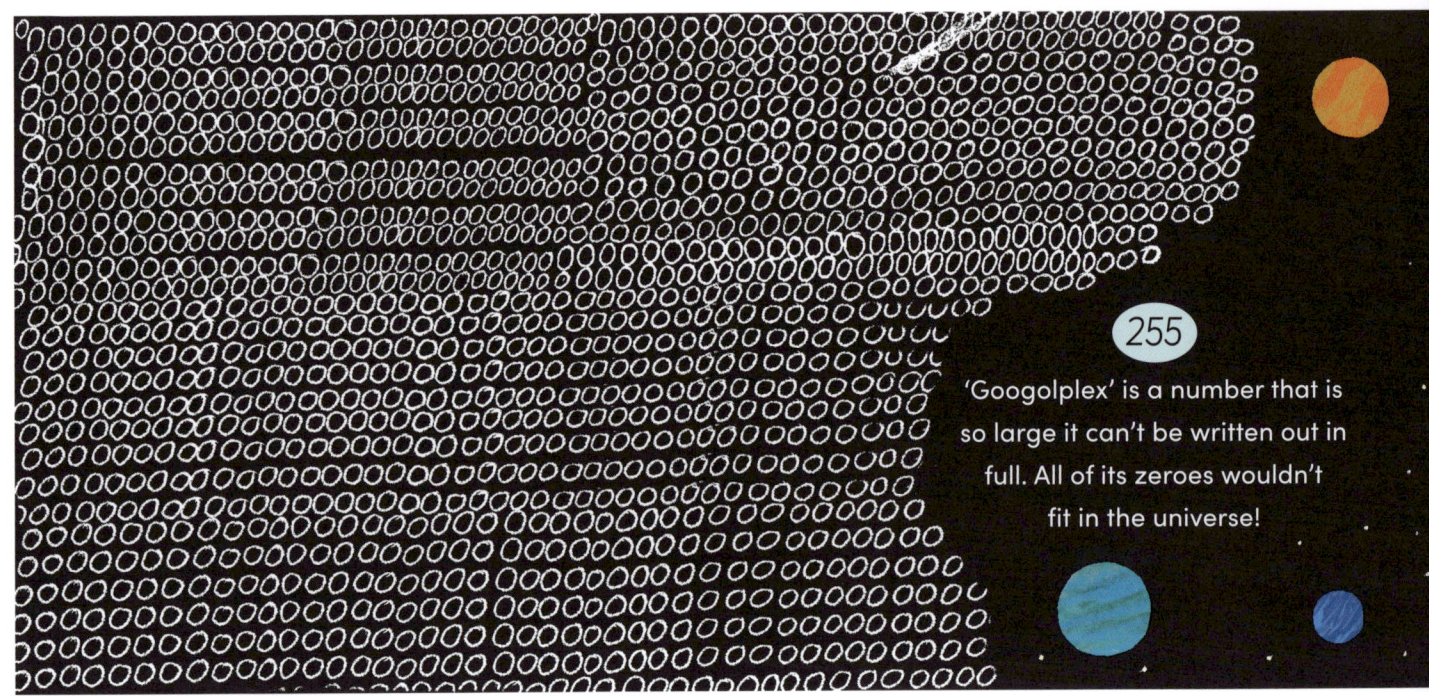

255

'Googolplex' is a number that is so large it can't be written out in full. All of its zeroes wouldn't fit in the universe!

256

Landline telephone numbers in Cape Canaveral, USA, where NASA's spacecraft are launched, all begin with the area code 321.

257

Crows can count out loud up to four.

258

Trees can sweat.

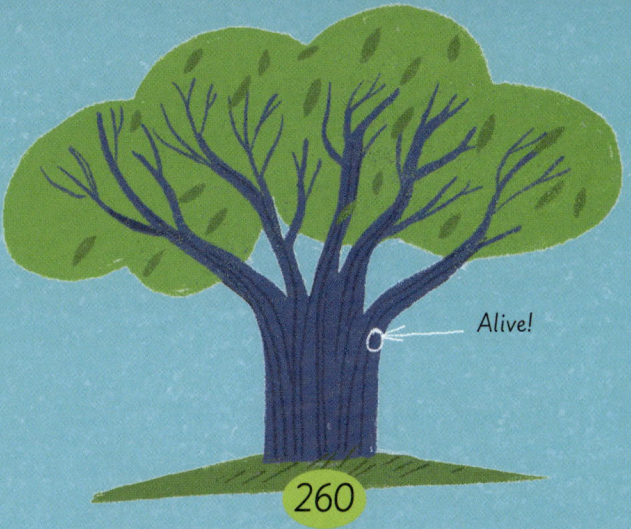

Alive!

260

Only one per cent of a mature tree is alive.

259

In the grounds of Syracuse University in New York, USA, there's a beautiful tree that grows 40 different types of fruit on its branches. Created by Professor Sam Van Aken, the 'Tree of 40 Fruit' was the first such tree to be grown. Every year the tree produces a range of fruit that you'd expect to find in a supermarket, including apricots, cherries, nectarines, plums and peaches.

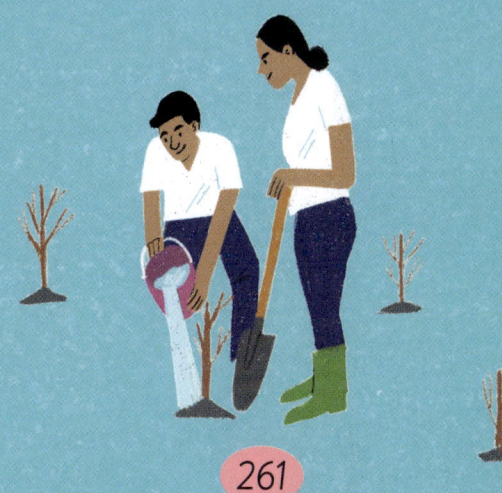

261

In just 12 hours in 2017, a team of around 1.5 million volunteers planted 66 million trees in India.

Who are you calling grass!?

262

Antarctica was so warm 53 million years ago that there were palm trees along its shore.

263

Technically palm trees aren't trees, but very tall grass.

264

Japanese scientists have invented a banana with edible peel, called the Mongee banana. In Japanese, 'mongee' is a slang word meaning 'incredible'.

265

Rhubarb develops so quickly in the dark (2.5 cm per day) that you can hear it creaking as it grows.

266

Children grow faster in the spring.

267

When they're enjoying a meal, gorillas make up happy songs to sing while they eat.

268

In 1872, Denmark replaced the letter Q with the letter K.

269

If you want to tell someone to leave you alone in Portuguese, you can say *vai pentear macacos*, which means 'go away and comb monkeys'.

270

If you stay at the Hotel Charleroi in Belgium and you feel lonely in your room, you can rent a goldfish for the night.

271

About a third of British grown-ups sleep with a cuddly toy.

272

An Ancient Roman politician called Lucius Licinius Crassus had a pet eel that he trained to come when he called it. He loved it so much he gave it necklaces and earrings to wear and held a grand funeral when it died.

273

The **gladiators** of Ancient Rome ate a mostly vegetarian diet. After exercising they drank a liquid made from the ash of burnt plants.

274

A pelican can gulp down a pigeon whole.

275

In Swiss supermarkets you can buy burgers made of insects.

Run for your lives!

276

The biggest chicken nugget ever made weighed 20.96 kilograms, which is about 115 times larger than a normal nugget, and nine times as big as the average chicken.

Mmm... the Romans make great bread!

277

French toast is older than France. The French used to call it 'Roman Bread'.

278

The inventor of the chocolate chip cookie, Ruth Wakefield, sold the recipe to the company Nestlé (for just $1!) on the condition that she would receive a lifetime's supply of chocolate.

279

People had been drinking tea for more than 4,500 years before someone invented the teabag.

280

Sheep were farmed for 3,000 years before anyone thought to use their wool.

281

The French **delicacy** of frogs' legs was eaten in England 8,000 years before it was enjoyed in France.

282

Wealthy Ancient Romans would treat their dinner guests to a delicacy of roast dormouse. One recipe said to sprinkle the mice with honey and poppy seeds; another said to stuff them with pork, pepper, fish sauce, nuts and their own guts.

283

The Ancient Greeks loved playing a game called *kottabos,* which consisted of flicking the dregs from their wine cups at a target in the middle of the room. The players reclined on couches that were arranged in a circle around the target, so if they missed they might hit each other instead.

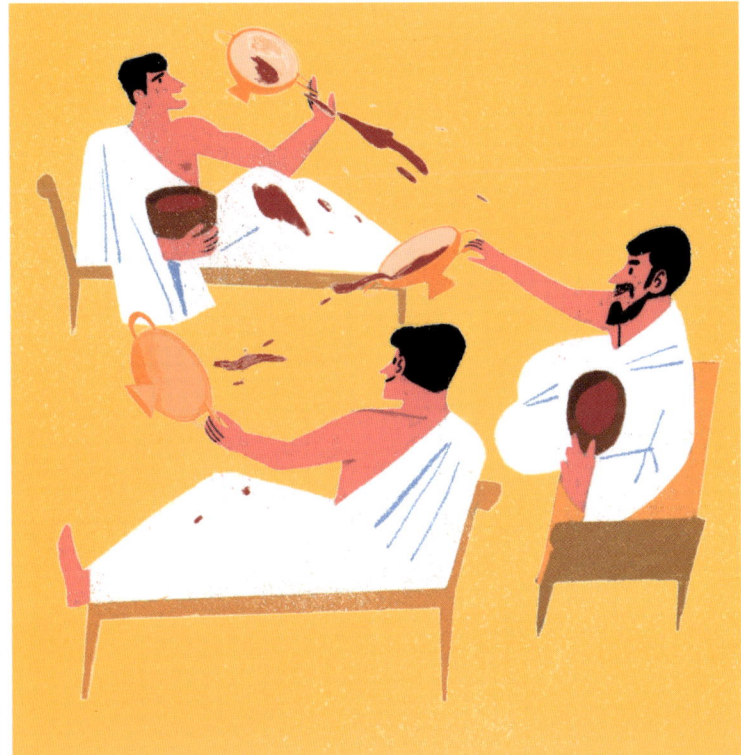

284

Herodorus of Megara was a famous trumpeter in Ancient Greece who won Olympic trumpet-blowing competitions ten times. He could even blow two trumpets at once.

285

Ancient Romans used wee as mouthwash.

286

The women of Ancient Rome used rotten leeches soaked in red wine to dye their hair black. For red hair dye they used animal fat mixed with beech tree ash. Some wealthy Romans even brightened their blonde hair with gold powder.

287

Today when people get married, guests might throw confetti or rice over them. In Ancient Rome, they threw walnuts.

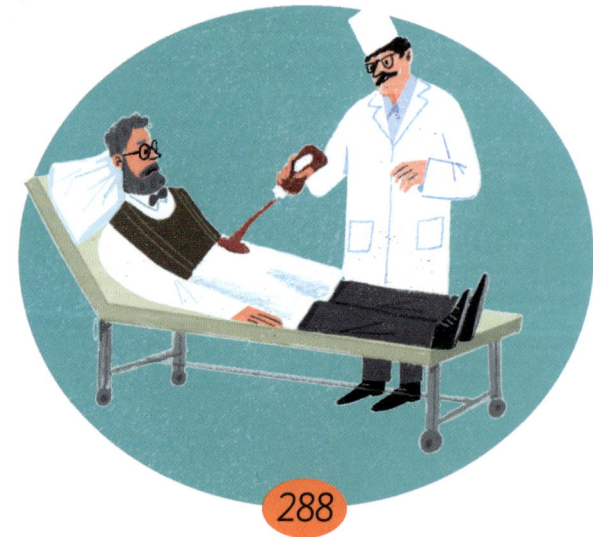

288

Tomato ketchup used to be sold in pill form as medicine for upset stomachs.

289
The Great Wall of China was built using sticky rice instead of cement to hold the bricks and stones together.

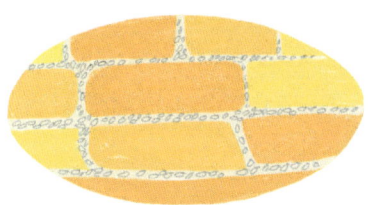

290
The longest sausage in the world was made in Romania in 2014. At 63 kilometres long and weighing 45 tonnes, it had to be exhibited in a supermarket car park. After it was shown off, it was donated to charity.

291
Just one bite from the lone star tick can cause you to develop a serious allergy to red meat for the rest of your life.

292
Chefs at a fast food company once tried to create bubblegum-flavoured broccoli, but the product never made it into the restaurants.

293
Lake Cerknica in Slovenia disappears every year. It's called an 'intermittent lake'. When it's full, it's the largest lake in the country at 6.1 metres deep. In summer, when there's less rain, the water drains into underground reservoirs.

294

The 'Carcross Desert' is a small area of sand dunes in Canada, measuring 2.6 square kilometres. In winter, the dunes are great for skiing and snowboarding.

295

The narrowest street in the world is Spreuerhofstraße in Reutlingen, Germany. It's only 31 cm wide at its narrowest point.

296

The Newby-McMahon Building in Wichita Falls, Texas, USA, is known as 'the world's littlest skyscraper'. From the plans, the townspeople thought it would be 480 feet tall, but the man who built it tricked them and only made it 480 *inches* tall. By the time people realized, he'd run away with the money!

297

Russia is so large that it spreads across 11 time zones. This means that when people in eastern regions of Russia are having breakfast, the people in western Russia are sitting down for dinner.

298
Today, New York City is nicknamed 'The Big Apple', but before that, some people called it 'The Big Onion', as there were so many layers to explore.

299
In the future, street lamps could be replaced with trees that glow in the dark. A Danish company is developing a bioluminescent tree. This is also what gives fireflies their glow.

300
Scientists recently discovered that humans glow in the dark. In fact, all living creatures produce a small amount of light made by the chemical reactions occurring inside their bodies.

301
There are about 100 known species of mushrooms that glow in the dark.

302
At Mosquito Bay on the Puerto Rican island of Vieques, the sea glows in the dark. The water is full of single-celled organisms called dinoflagellates that glow bright blue when you touch them.

303

Australia has several lakes that are bright pink. They get their rosy colour from **microbes** in the water.

304

In Racetrack Valley, Nevada, USA, there are rocks that seem to move by themselves across the desert floor. This happens when ice forms on the ground, and the wind pushes the stones along the slippery surface.

305

Every summer, the city of Yoro in Honduras holds the Festival of the Rain of Fish to celebrate the phenomenon of fish falling from the sky, which they say can happen as often as four times a year.

306

A 'thunder-plump' is an old term used in Scotland and Northern Ireland for a sudden burst of rain. A 'cow-quaker' describes a thunder-plump that falls in May.

307

To predict the weather, forecasters use supercomputers that process about 2.8 quadrillion mathematical calculations per second.

308

The winds in an average hurricane are strong enough to produce about 1.5 **trillion** watts of energy. This could power half the world for an entire year.

309

The USA uses more electricity just for air-conditioning than the continent of Africa uses for everything.

310

The geographical centre of North America is a town called Center. It's a weird coincidence – it was named years ago for a totally unrelated reason!

What a crazy coincidence!

311

There's a town in Arizona, USA, called Nothing. No one lives there. It once had four people, but it was abandoned in 2005.

312

The town of Snowflake, Arizona, USA, was named by the men who founded it in 1878 – Erastus Snow and William Flake.

313

There's a town in Nebraska, USA, called Monowi. Only one person lives there. She works as the mayor, bartender and librarian.

314

People in La Laguna, Tenerife, can speak backwards! A local barber invented the *Verres* language in the 1930s to have fun confusing his customers and it caught on.

Woh trohs ta eht pot, ris?

79

315

In the 19th century in New York City, every year at 9 a.m. on 1 May, thousands of residents would all move house at the same time. This was because landlords raised the rent on this day, forcing people to find cheaper places to live.

316

The people of the Yap Islands in Micronesia have a form of stone money called *rai* that they still use for ceremonial transactions. The doughnut-shaped stone 'coins' can be as large as four metres in diameter.

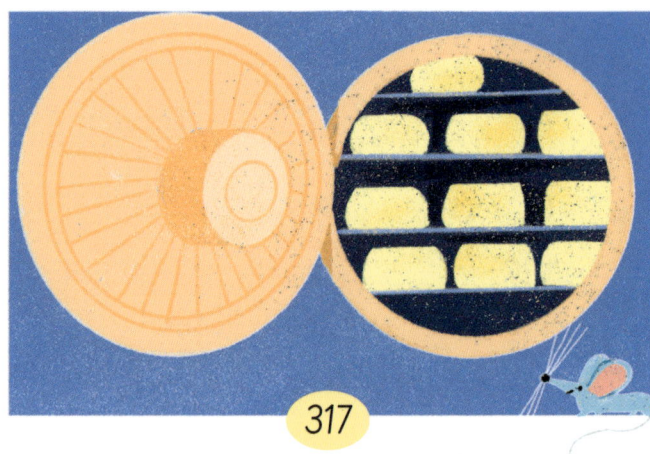

317

There's a bank in Italy where you can pay with cheese. Since 1953, Credito Emiliano in northern Italy has lent dairy farmers money in exchange for wheels of parmesan cheese, which the bank keeps in air-conditioned vaults.

318

In Italy 500 years ago, when wine went bad people thought it was because a witch had weed in it.

319

In the Middle Ages, doctors would try to diagnose illnesses by smelling and tasting the patient's wee.

320

The smell of the durian fruit is considered one of the worst smells in the world. The fruit has such a bad stink that in some countries, such as Malaysia and Thailand, it's illegal to take it on public transport.

321

In 1931, some farmers in New Zealand were shocked when their trousers burst into flames. It turned out they had used a popular weedkiller that could ignite itself.

322

Owing to a by-law passed in 1800, it was technically illegal for Parisian women to wear trousers. The regulation was finally legally dropped in 2013.

323

There is vitamin B12 in rainwater, and vitamin A in human tears.

324
Some birds dream about singing.

325
Rats dream about places they want to explore.

326
There is a bird native to the Galápagos Islands called the vampire ground finch. It's named after its habit of pecking the skin and drinking the blood of certain types of sea birds when it runs out of food.

327
Flamingos are born white or grey, and slowly turn pink as they get older.

328
A giant gourami fish at an aquarium in London once turned pink after staff fed it prawn cocktail flavoured crisps.

329
An ant's sense of smell is more sensitive than a dog's.

330
Trap-jaw ants smell like chocolate when they're irritated. Citronella ants smell like lemons if they feel threatened.

331
King Frederick William I of Prussia was so obsessed with giants that he decided to make a unit of soldiers who were fantastically tall to frighten his enemies. The regiment of 'Potsdam Giants' was founded in 1675, and only the tallest men in the country were hired. The king even encouraged his 'giants' to marry exceedingly tall women, so that they would have extra-tall children.

332
A Hungarian girl named Jadwiga was only about ten years old when she was made King of Poland in 1384 (at that time 'King' was used for male and female rulers).

333

Queen Victoria had a brooch and earrings made from her children's baby teeth.

Don't tell anyone my real name!

334

Queen Victoria's first name was actually Alexandrina.

335

Queen Victoria owned a bulletproof parasol and two tricycles.

336

In 18th-century Europe, people used miniature cannons to signal when it was noon. A magnifying glass focused the midday sun's rays, lighting the gunpowder, and making the cannon fire with a BANG.

337

A popular game in England from the 16th century was Snapdragon, in which a bowl of raisins and brandy was set on fire. The players had to try to eat the raisins without burning themselves.

338

Human chess is a life-size game of chess in which people act as the pieces, standing on a giant game board. Since 1454, a game of human chess has been played every two years in the Italian city of Marostica, featuring cannons, people on horseback and soldiers in uniform.

339

Vikings were buried with board games so they wouldn't get bored in the afterlife.

340

King Olaf Tryggvason of Norway (who reigned about CE 995–1000) liked to run around on the oars of his Viking ship while it was being rowed!

341

A useful god to pray to in Ancient Rome was Cardea, who was the goddess of door hinges and handles. It was her job to stop evil spirits and monsters from entering people's houses.

342

The Aztec people of South America loved popcorn so much that they wore popcorn headdresses and necklaces for ceremonial dances.

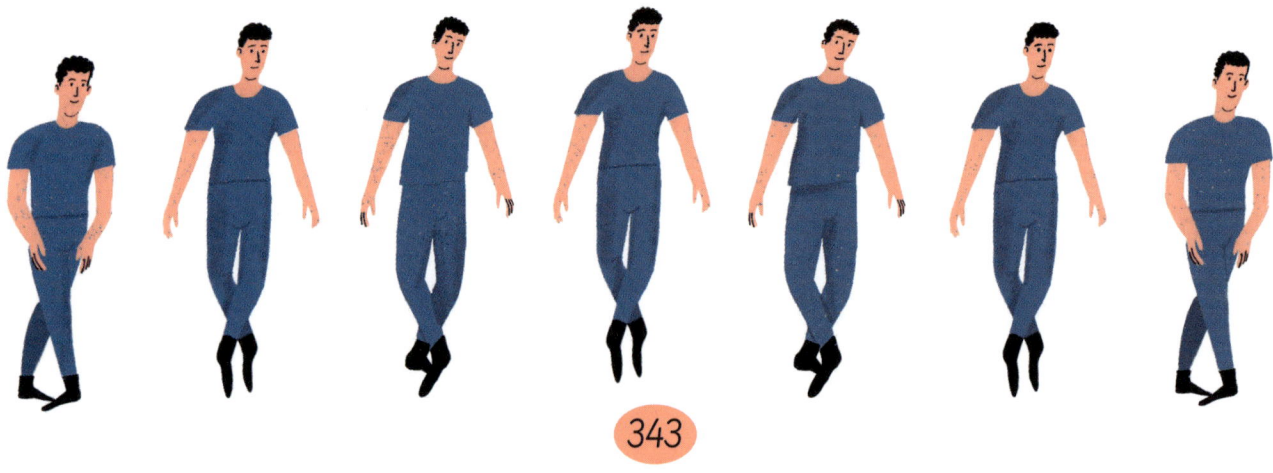

343

In 1973, the English dancer Wayne Sleep became the first person to successfully perform an *entrechat douze*, a ballet jump in which he crossed and uncrossed his straight legs *five times in one leap*.

  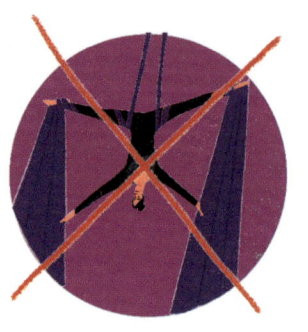 

344

While he was President of Turkmenistan (1991–2006), Saparmurat Niyazov outlawed ballet, gold teeth, the circus, listening to car radios, and growing beards or having long hair.

345

In Venice, Italy, there was an old tradition in which the *doge* (a title similar to 'duke') of the city got married to the Adriatic Sea by throwing a gold ring into its waters. The yearly custom was started as a way of showing enemies that Venice had the sea on its side. The ceremony still happens today, with the city's mayor taking the doge's role.

346

There is a tradition among the Tidung people, **indigenous** to Kalimantan in Indonesia, in which newly married couples aren't allowed to use the bathroom for three days after their wedding.

347

In Viking mythology, Freyja, the wife of Odr, was the goddess of marriage. She also looked after brave warriors who died in battle. But a lot of her time was spent searching the Earth for her wandering husband, crying tears of red gold as she rode her chariot pulled by cats.

348

There was an Ancient Greek sea goddess called Doris. Her name comes from the Greek word for 'gift'.

349

The world's most expensive cheese is Pule cheese, which is made in Serbia from donkeys' milk. It costs so much money because it takes lots more milk, time and effort to make than other cheeses.

350

In Kenya, some cows have giant eyes painted on their bottoms to stop lions from attacking them. It works!

351

In South Africa, some cows are given reflective ear tags (like shiny earrings!) so that drivers can see them at night.

352

Cows produce five times as much **saliva** as milk per day.

353

Before refrigerators existed, people in Russia and Finland kept their milk fresh by putting a live frog in it.

354

The Vatican, where the Pope lives, keeps its buildings white by painting the exterior walls with milk from the Pope's own herd of cows.

355

In 2020, a Siberian farmer had the idea of keeping his cows warm by strapping woolly bras around their udders.

Winter

Summer

356

In the vast Russian region of Siberia, it's so cold in winter that spruce and pine trees have learned to survive temperatures of −60°C by temporarily turning their tissue to glass. As it gets warmer later in the year, they start to thaw and wake up.

357

To help a tortoise **hibernate** over winter, you can put it in a refrigerator. It's important to keep it away from food and open the door regularly to let fresh air in.

Summer babies

You snooze, you lose!

Winter baby

358

The chances are that babies born in a winter month start crawling about five weeks earlier than their friends born in the summer.

359

Fake snow in old black and white films was made by painting cornflakes white.

360

There is a tiny bit of dust at the heart of every snowflake.

361

Scientists think there could be about 10 million woolly mammoths preserved under the ice in the Arctic.

362
In Britain, people use enough wrapping paper in one year to gift-wrap the Moon.

363
The first Christmas crackers were called 'Bangs of Expectation'. They were invented by a sweet-maker called Tom Smith as a way of selling French-style sweets which came wrapped in twisted paper. The exploding bang was added by Smith's brother, who had learnt the trick while working for magicians.

364
Rudolph the Red-Nosed Reindeer is a girl, as are all the other reindeer that pull Santa's sleigh. We know this because the reindeer are always shown as having antlers. Male reindeer use their antlers to fight each other during the autumn breeding season, so by Christmas they have cast them off. Only females keep their antlers through the winter period.

365

The world's tallest Christmas tree is taller than the Statue of Liberty! The Douglas fir is the most popular type of Christmas tree, and the tallest Douglas fir in the world is the Doerner Fir in Oregon, USA, standing at 99.7 metres. The tree doesn't have branches until about 60 metres up, so to climb it, people use crossbows or giant slingshots to throw up their climbing ropes. The tree is so tall that it has its own ecosystems of animals at the top. There are endangered spotted owls, flying squirrels, red tree voles, and even clouded salamanders living up there without ever coming down to the ground.

366

Every four years something strange happens to our calendar: we get an extra day, 29 February. This is because a year, which is the time it takes for the Earth to revolve around the Sun, isn't exactly 365 days, but 365 days and nearly 6 hours. This means that after four years we have an extra 24 hours, and so we add a day into the calendar to account for it. This special year of 366 days is called a leap year.

Glossary

Avatar – in a computer game, this is the character that the player controls

Barbarian – a word for a person the Ancient Romans and Ancient Greeks thought was uncivilized

Biofuel – a fuel that is made from recently living matter, not oil

Black hole – a region in space where gravity is so strong that nothing can escape, not even light

Buoyant – able to float

Carnivore – an animal or plant that eats meat

Constellation – a group of stars that form a recognizable pattern

Delicacy – an expensive treat

Dense – the closer something's parts are compacted together, the denser it is

Evolution – the process by which living things develop from earlier forms of life

Galaxy – a huge system of billions of stars, planets, gas and dust drawn together by gravity

Gladiator – a man trained to fight against other men and animals in an arena in Ancient Rome

Glory – a rainbow pattern created by light passing through a narrow space

Gravity – the force by which a planet or other body draws objects toward its centre

Hibernate – when an animal slows its heart rate to sleep through the winter

Indigenous – existing naturally, or having always lived, in a place

Lava – hot molten rock that bursts out from the inside of the Earth

Mangrove – a shrub or tree that mainly grows in salt water

Microbe – a very tiny living thing that can't be seen with the naked eye

Plasma – after liquid, gas and solid, plasma is the fourth state of matter. It's a very hot gas with a lot more energy than the other three states

Protein – molecules in the body that build, maintain and replace tissue like muscles

Prototype – the first test model of a new design

Pseudonym – a fake name that a writer uses to hide their true identity

Rover – a robotic vehicle that is used to explore a planet or moon while being controlled on Earth

Saliva – the clear liquid in your mouth otherwise known as spit

Savoury – a food or dish that is full of salty or spicy flavour

Supernova – the explosion of a star

Tendons – cords of tissue in the body that connect the ends of muscle to a bone or other part of the body

Thorax – the central body region of an insect

Trillion – a trillion is 1,000,000,000,000, or one million million

Venom – a poisonous substance that some animals inject into prey with a bite or sting

About the author

Edward Brooke-Hitching worked for a long time as a 'QI Elf' (a fact-hunter and scriptwriter for the BBC television show QI) before writing bestselling works of curious history and science for adults and children. Having grown up in a rare-book shop, he now lives in his own dusty heap of old paintings, books and maps in the Berkshire countryside with his red Labrador, Annie Jump Cannon. His favourite fact is that sharks are older than trees. His advice for fact-finding is to be suspicious and find at least three different sources that confirm the fact is true, as there is a lot of made-up information out there!

About the illustrator

Oksana Drachkovska was born in Chernivtsi, Ukraine, in 1987. She grew up in Chernivtsi before moving to study at an art college in the Carpathians, followed by the Academy of Fine Arts in Lviv. She is now based in Barcelona. Her sources of inspiration are diverse, sometimes even unconventional – trees, the sea, the ocean, birds and clouds. Observing people is also a significant source of inspiration for Oksana, as each encounter provides her with a deeper understanding of herself. She enjoys playing with metaphors and is someone who finds it easier to think on paper.